Sumati's Odyssey:

A journey through life, love and the universe

Poornima Dayal

ZORBA BOOKS

ZORBA BOOKS

Published by Zorba Books, August 2025
Website: www.zorbabooks.com
Email: info@zorbabooks.com
Author Name: Poornima Dayal

Title: Sumati's Odyssey: A journey through life, love and the universe

Printbook ISBN: 978-93-5896-108-9
Ebook ISBN: 978-93-5896 515 5

Zorba Books Pvt. Ltd. (opc)
Sushant Arcade,
Next to Courtyard Marriot,
Sushant Lok 1, Gurgaon – 122009, India

Printed in India

TABLE OF CONTENTS

PREFACE

As I sit down to share the story (a fictional narrative) of Sumati's Odyssey – I am reminded of my own journey—one that has been as much inward as outward, as much a quest for meaning as it is a celebration of life's incredible mysteries.

Like many, I once found myself caught in the whirlwind of modern life—chasing success, material comforts and fleeting pleasures, while feeling an inexplicable emptiness echo within. It was only through quiet moments of reflection, encounters with nature's sacred beauty and the stories of countless souls I met along the way that I began to understand the profound truth: the Divine is not distant, but is woven into the very fabric of life and the universe, waiting patiently for us to recognize His magnificent presence.

This novel is inspired by the universal journey of seeking—of exploring the vastness of the world and ultimately, the depths of our own hearts. It is a reflection of my own realizations: that the greatest, lasting treasures lie not in distant lands or in momentary material pleasures but in the divine love that resides within us all. Through Sumati's travels and transformations, I hope to inspire readers to listen to their inner voice, to find felicity in everyday moments and to embrace the harmony of life with an open heart.

Writing this story has been a pilgrimage—a return to my own roots, a rediscovery of faith, hope and unconditional love. It has taught me that the path to understanding oneself is never linear but a beautiful, unfolding journey of surrender, love and joy.

May this story serve as a gentle reminder: no matter where life takes us, the divine is always near, whispering in the wind, shining in the stars and dancing within our souls. All we need is the courage to listen, the humility to learn and the love to embrace ourselves—and each other—in the sacredness of life.

With love and thanks,
Poornima Dayal

ACKNOWLEDGMENT

I am grateful to the Divine for guiding me through this fictional narrative. I also thank my husband, my son, my mother and my loving pet, without their support writing this book would not have possible.

I am grateful to the Lord for all those moments or situations in my life which have steered me to such ideas and thoughts.

Importantly, thank you readers, for taking out the time to pick this book.

INTRODUCTION

Imagine a world where the boundaries between the seen and unseen blur, where every moment holds a whisper of the Divine and the journey inward becomes the greatest adventure of all. 'Sumati's Odyssey' beckons you into such a realm—a story of one woman's quest to find her true self amidst everyday life' and beauty.

As you turn these pages, you'll follow Sumati's footsteps across mystical landscapes, encounter characters whose lives inspire her and assist her in discovering the universal truth that sometimes, the greatest treasures are hidden within. This isn't just a story about travel or discovery; it's an invitation to reflect on your own path, to listen to the quiet voice of your soul and to realize that the divine presence within us all is waiting to be realised.

Are you ready to embark on a journey that could change the way you see yourself and the world? Let's begin.

CHAPTER 1

THE SEEKER

Mumbai was alive with its own heartbeat—an unceasing rhythm of honking horns, street vendors calling out, the distant chanting of temple bells and the monsoon rain tapping against the window panes. But inside Sumati's modest apartment, amidst a jumble of books, incense sticks and flickering candles, a different kind of storm brewed.

She sat cross-legged on her balcony, wrapped in a soft, printed shawl gazing up at the darkened sky. The clouds were thick, heavy with rain, swirling in wild patterns that seemed to mirror her restless thoughts. Her eyes traced the flickering stars—tiny, glistening specks of light in the vast open sky—and she wondered about the universe beyond.

Sumati is a 42 year old woman of graceful presence, with a stature that commands quiet admiration. She stands about 5 feet 5 inches tall, her slender frame embodying a delicate strength. Her skin is a warm, honeyed tone, reflecting a life filled with both resilience and serenity. Her eyes are large and chestnut brown that seem to hold centuries of compassion. Her thick, dark curly hair is rolled into a perfect bun.

"There's so much I don't see," she mused softly, her voice blending with the distant hum of the city. Even though the city's murmur was familiar and comforting, her heart yearned for something else—something deeper, more eternal.

Despite the whirl of her busy city life—corporate meetings, deadlines, social obligations—her heart often drifted to her family. She loved her husband Arjun, an empathetic artist whose gentle nature complemented her own quiet strength. Their mornings were filled with shared coffee, soft conversations about dreams and hopes and quiet moments of understanding. Her children, Riya and Aman, brought her immeasurable joy—Aman's innocent laughter, Riya's curious questions, their warm hugs and their unconditional love made her heart swell.

Tonight, as she sat on her balcony, her thoughts wandered to her family. She gently touched her brass idol of Lord Shiva and Parvati sitting on her windowsill, their serene faces seeming to hold the secrets she longed to understand. "Is there more they wish to tell?" she whispered softly, feeling tears threaten to spill. But she quickly brushed them away, swallowing her emotion. She was used to hiding her vulnerability behind a brave, composed exterior.

Her husband Arjun caught her immersed in thought. Quietly sitting besides her, placing a reassuring hand on her shoulder. "You look far away, Sumati," he said softly. She smiled, leaning into his warmth, grateful for his quiet understanding. "There's so much in this city that I love," she replied, her voice tinged with affection. "But there's also a part of me that yearns for something more—something beyond the skyline, beyond the daily city life.”

Her love for Mumbai was deep-rooted. The city’s vibrant energy, its endless possibilities and its unbreakable spirit fueled her ambition. Yet, beneath her success and her love for her home, a restless craving stirred—a desire to see the world, to breathe in new landscapes and to discover the divine truths hidden in distant lands.

She reached out and gently touched a large book—a carefully crafted and designed volume titled 'The Wonders of the Universe'—which had been lying on a white, marble shelf carefully placed in her elegant living room. She had bought the book months ago during a fleeting moment of curiosity but hadn’t yet read past the first few pages.

Now, she opened it with her slender fingers. The pages crackled softly, releasing a faint glimpse of distant galaxies. The words shimmered as she read:

"The universe is a divine dance—a cosmic symphony where stars are the notes and galaxies are the melodies. Every atom in your body resonates with the rhythm of creation."

Her breath caught. She closed her eyes, letting the words seep into her soul. “Could there be a connection between this vast universe and the quiet divine within me?” she wondered.

That night, as Mumbai’s monsoon raged outside, Sumati made a silent vow. “I will find out. I will explore the world, not just with my feet but with my heart and soul.”

The next morning, as sunlight broke through the clouds, she felt a new sense of purpose stirring within her. Her restless spirit was awakening.

Later that evening, as her family gathered for dinner—with Arjun's soft voice blending with the laughter of Riya and Aman—Sumati's heart was filled with gratitude. Her children's innocent chatter about their day, her husband's tender glances and the warmth of home grounded her even as her mind wandered to distant horizons.

One evening, she sat with Arjun in their cozy living room, sketching ideas for her upcoming art exhibition.

Arjun was a 43-year-old man of quiet strength and gentle demeanor, his presence understated yet compelling. His face was framed by thick, black hair that often fell slightly over his forehead, giving him a thoughtful, contemplative look. His eyes, deep and almond-shaped, held a calm, piercing gaze—like a still lake that reflected kindness. A strong jawline and a hint of stubble added to his understated masculinity, despite his reserved exterior, he possessed an unwavering inner strength and a profound sense of responsibility, especially towards his family.

He paused, looking at her with love in his eyes. "You've been dreaming of a trip for a long time," he said softly. "Go and find what you're searching for. We'll be here, waiting for you my darling, proud of your courage."

Riya and Aman, listening from nearby, nodded enthusiastically. "Mama, will you bring us back a star?"

Aman asked, eyes wide with wonder. Riya added, "And a snowflake from the mountains?"

Sumati's heart melted. She hugged her children close, feeling their love anchor her. "I promise," she whispered. "This journey is for all of us—for the love of discovery and the love within our hearts."

Sumati's children were lively and curious, each carrying a unique sparkle in their eyes. Her eldest, Aman was ten years old—a boy with an adventurous streak and quick wit. He loved exploring the outdoors, often wandering into the playgrounds with his friends and always eager for the next discovery. His favorite pastime was storytelling, weaving fantastic tales from his imagination that captivated everyone around him.

Her daughter, Riya, was eight, gentle and observant. She had a love for art and spent hours sketching flowers, birds and scenes from nature. Both children shared a bond of innocence and wonder, their playful laughter and curious minds filling their home with warmth and light.

Her love for Mumbai and her family intertwined with her yearning for adventure. She knew that her travels would not only quench her curiosity but also deepen her understanding of herself, her belief and the divine dance that connects all living beings.

And so, with her loved ones' blessings and her heart brimming with hope, Sumati prepared for her voyage—ready to explore the splendors of the world, driven by the divine spark within her.

The next morning, as sunlight broke through the clouds, she felt a new sense of purpose stirring within her. She was undoubtedly happy and looking forward.

CHAPTER 2

NEW ZEALAND'S EMBRACE

The days leading up to her departure were filled with a whirlwind of activity. Sumati packed her bags thoughtfully, each item chosen with care—comfortable hiking shoes, a journal, meditation cushions, warm layers for the cool mountain air and her favorite books on spirituality.

Her friends teased her about her sudden burst of adventure. "Mumbai to New Zealand? Isn't that a bit much for a soul-searching trip?" her best friend Anjali joked, smiling. Sumati only nodded softly, her eyes shining with quiet determination.

She spent evenings browsing travel blogs, reading about the landscapes she would soon see—fiords carved by ancient glaciers, lush forests echoing with bird songs and serene lakes shimmering under mountain shadows. She booked her flights, arranged her accommodations in Queenstown and even enrolled in a short meditation retreat in Fiordland. Even her office was kind enough to grant her the much deserved annual leave.

"This journey is for me," she whispered each night, feeling the weight of her old life loosen. Her heart fluttered with anticipation and a gentle nervousness.

The flight was long but uneventful. As the airplane descended into Queenstown, her heart soared at the sight of the rugged mountains and sparkling lakes stretching endlessly below. The crisp mountain air greeted her as she stepped off the plane, a welcome balm after the humid Mumbai monsoon.

Her first days in New Zealand were a gentle awakening. She wandered through the quaint town, marveling at the blend of modern charm and untouched wilderness. At a local café, she sipped on herbal tea, gazing out at the snow-capped peaks that seemed to touch the sky.

One morning, she set out for her first trek—an ascent into the Fiordland National Park. The trail snaked through dense forests, moss-covered trees towering above her, their leaves whispering stories in the breeze. As she climbed higher, the scenery transformed: waterfalls cascading from cliffs, the scent of pine and damp earth filling her senses.

Reaching a quiet lakeside nestled among mountains, Sumati paused. The lake's surface was perfectly still, reflecting the sky and surrounding peaks like a giant mirror. She sat on a wooden bench, her legs dangling on a smooth stone slab, closing her eyes.

In that silence, she felt a deep connection—an almost electric current flowing from the earth through her body into the universe. Her breath slowed, and she entered a meditative state, feeling the serene energy of the mountains and lakes.

"This is the divine within me," she thought. "Nature is a mirror of my inner universe."

She opened her journal and scribbled her thoughts:

"In the stillness of this lake, I sense the divine pulse—an eternal rhythm that connects all living things. I am a part of this cosmic dance."

Each day, she returned to this practice, meditating by waterfalls, under ancient trees and beside tranquil lakes. The mountains seemed to whisper truths about patience, resilience and love—lessons she carried deep within her.

During her explorations, Sumati met local Maori tribesmen and fellow travelers. An elderly Maori woman named Tui shared stories of their ancient heritage and of the culture of their land and the sacredness of nature. Her gentle voice spoke of the universe's magic and how every element, from the smallest pebble to the highest mountain, embodies divine energy.

Tui handed Sumati a carved pendant symbolizing the connection between earth, water, fire and air. "Wear this," she said softly, " her nimble fingers handing it over gingerly to Sumati.

Its pristine blue stone gave Sumati a sense of belonging – belonging to this Universe, which is filled with boundless love.

In the mountains, she also encountered a group of hikers from around the world. They exchanged stories of their journeys and in those shared moments, Sumati realized that her quest was universal—a search for divine connection that transcended borders and languages.

One evening, as she watched the sunset paint the sky in hues of orange and pink, Sumati felt a profound shift within her. Her restless mind had quieted, replaced by a deep sense of calm.

She thought about her journey from Mumbai's busy life to this tranquil wilderness. She understood that the revered Lord was not distant— He was in her breath, in the wind, in the stillness of the lake.

"I am part of this wonderful universe," she whispered, eyes shining with tears of joy. "Am I not fortunate?"

Her journal now brimmed with reflections, sketches of mountains and notes on her spiritual insights. She felt a warm glow of gratitude—her quest was just beginning and the universe was unfolding its secrets before her.

CHAPTER 3

WHISPERING WINDS AND THE CALL OF THE MOUNTAINS

The crisp air in Queenstown carried a gentle melody—the whispering winds that seemed to call her name. Every dawn, she woke with a sense of anticipation, eager to explore more of the mountain trails, lakes and forests. Her heart was light, her spirit buoyant.

One morning, she decided to hike up to the Remarkables, a mountain range renowned for their jagged peaks. The trail was steep but invigorating, each step a prayer of gratitude for the beauty surrounding her. She marveled at the way the sunlight painted the rocks in hues of gold and cadmium yellow, casting long shadows that danced across the landscape.

As she reached a ridge overlooking a vast valley, she paused, gazing out at the sprawling wilderness below. The mountains seemed to embrace her, their ancient presence a testament to resilience and timeless wisdom.

"Nature's resilience inspires me," she thought, smiling. "Just like these mountains, I too can stand tall through storms."

She closed her eyes, took a deep breath, and felt the divine energy flowing through her—like a gentle stream that nourished her soul.

Back at her cozy lodge, Sumati settled into her meditation spot—facing the window that framed the mountains. She lit her favorite 'Rose' incense sticks, their fragrance mirroring the fragrance of hope and joy within her. She closed her eyes and sank into a deep meditation, focusing on her breath.

In that moment, she envisioned the universe as a vast, loving consciousness—an infinite ocean of light. She felt her heart expand, radiating warmth and compassion, connecting her to everything around her.

“Love is our true nature," she whispered inwardly. “Every leaf, every star, every breath— is a part of this marvellous love.”

Her optimism grew sharper, like the morning sun piercing through clouds. She saw herself as a vessel of light, carrying love and hope into the world.

After a while, Sumati found herself sitting by the window, a sketchbook resting on her lap. She loved painting as well, just like her husband, Arjun and daughter Riya.The breathtaking majesty of the mountains stretched endlessly before her, their snow-capped peaks piercing the clear blue sky. Inspired, she pulled out her pencils and began to sketch, capturing the rugged beauty with fine strokes. Her hand moved instinctively, trying to preserve the serenity of the scene—the jagged edges of the cliffs, the distant shimmer of a waterfall and the lush greenery that clung to the mountain slopes.

As her sketch took shape, She felt completely immersed in the moment, as if the mountains were whispering stories only she could hear. After completing the outline, she reached for her set of soft pastels—vivid shades of blue, green and white. Carefully, she filled in her drawing, blending colors to bring the scene alive. The snow glistened with icy whites and pale blues, while the greenery was vibrant and lush. The sky, a soft gradient of dawn, transitioned seamlessly into the mountain shadows.

When she finally closed her pastel box and looked at her work, a warm smile spread across her face. The drawing was simple yet enchanting, capturing the essence of the majestic landscape. She held the sketchbook close, feeling a sense of accomplishment . That quiet morning, with the mountains as her muse, Sumati rediscovered her love for art and the simple pleasures of observing the world around her. It was a moment of pure happiness—one she would cherish forever.

The next day she volunteered at a local community garden, planting seedlings and sharing smiles with the villagers. The Maori elders told stories of how caring for the land was akin to caring for one's self. Sumati listened intently, feeling a kinship with their deep respect for nature's sacredness.

She realized that her journey was not only about seeking the truth but also about nurturing love and kindness—gifts she could bring back to her city life.

Later, she sat beneath a giant pohutukawa tree, its crimson flowers blooming vibrantly. She closed her eyes, feeling the heartbeat of the earth beneath her. Her heart filled with gratitude for this moment of pure connection.

“Every act of kindness plants a seed,” she mused,“and love is the most powerful flower of all.”

One breezy evening, she stood on the edge of Lake Wakatipu, watching the water ripple gently in the wind. The sky was painted in shades of violet and orange. As she inhaled the cool air, she felt a profound clarity: her inner world was blossoming, mirroring the beauty of the landscape.

A sudden gust of wind swept around her, carrying with it the scent of pine and wildflowers. She lifted her face to the sky, arms open wide, embracing the universe’s endless love.

“The wind carries my hopes,” she whispered, “and my heart is open to all its blessings.”

Her smile was radiant. She knew her optimism was a gift—a light that could brighten even the faintest corners. She thanked the Almighty for this gift.

That night her heart was eager to connect with her family back home and she retrieved her phone from her bag. With an enthusiastic touch she pressed the buttons on the screen and waited as it dialed.

“Hello, my loves,” she whispered softly, her voice carrying a mixture of warmth and longing.

On the other end, Arjun's familiar voice greeted her with a gentle laugh. "Sumati! darling, how are you? We've been waiting for your call all day."

"I'm good, Arjun," she replied, her eyes sparkling as she looked out over the tranquil lake. "It's breathtaking here—absolutely mesmerizing. The mountains are towering and the lakes are like glass, reflecting the sky and the clouds. I've finished an incredible trek through Fiordland's lush forests and waterfalls. It's like stepping into a fairy tale."

"Oh, that sounds wonderful," Arjun said, his tone filled with curiosity. "Tell me everything. How's the weather? Are you feeling inspired?"

"I'm feeling alive," Sumati said with a soft laugh. "The weather is perfect—bright sunshine with a cool breeze that makes everything shimmer. As I walked through the woods, I could hear the whisper of the wind, like nature's own lullaby. The lakes here are so still—they feel like portals to another world, a place where time slows down and the divine feels closer."

She paused, taking a deep breath, then continued, "Today, I wandered along the edge of Lake. It's so serene—like the earth's heart beating softly beneath the surface. I sat on a wooden dock, just watching the water ripple gently as the wind brushed past. I felt as if I was part of the divine—every wave, every gust of wind, a melody of life."

"Wow, sweetheart," Arjun responded, admiration evident in his voice. "You always had a poetic soul, but hearing you describe it makes me see it with new eyes. I wish I could be there with you, sitting by the lake, feeling the same."

"I wish you were here too," Sumati said softly. "But I carry you all in my heart. Riya and Aman are doing well, I hope? Tell me about them."

"Oh, they're as lively as ever," Arjun chuckled. "Riya is busy with her art assignments and dreaming up new projects. She's always full of ideas, sketching away in her notebook. Aman is happy—his laughter is contagious. Yesterday, he and Riya were playing in the nearby park, chasing each other around, pretending to be explorers in a jungle. They're so full of energy, it's like they're little sparks of joy."

"That's so lovely," Sumati said, her voice melting with tenderness. "Tell them I miss their giggles and their silly stories. I wish I could see their faces as they run and play, just like at home."

"They're doing just fine," Arjun assured her. "In fact, they keep asking about you—Aman wants to know if you've found a new star to bring back and Riya keeps asking if she can draw the mountains you've described. They're excited to hear all about New Zealand when you come back. And don't worry, everything is peaceful here. The house is lively with their games and your favorite music, songs from the film 'Yadon ki Barat', keep playing in the background."

"I'm so grateful," Sumati whispered, her eyes shining with emotion. "It warms my heart to hear that everyone is happy. I miss them terribly, but I also feel so alive here—like I'm reconnecting with God in a way I never imagined."

"That's beautiful, my love," Arjun said softly, his voice filled with affection. "Tell me more about your day. What else did you see or feel?"

"I spent the morning exploring Queenstown's charming streets," she began, her voice animated. "The town is nestled between the mountains and the lake and every corner seems to whisper stories of ancient explorers. I visited a cozy café overlooking the water—sipping herbal tea, watching the kayakers paddle past and the mountains standing tall like silent guardians. It's as if the landscape itself is a teacher, reminding me of strength and the love that sustains everything."

She paused, a slight smile on her lips. "Then, I took a boat across Lake Wakatipu, drifting quietly while the mountains reflected on the water's surface. I closed my eyes for a moment, feeling the gentle rocking of the boat, and I could sense the divine energy flowing through the earth, through me—connecting everything in a sacred web. I felt as if the mountains, the lakes, the wind—they're all part of the same, just like us."

"Sumati," Arjun said tenderly, "hearing you describe these places makes me feel like I'm right there with you.

Your words paint a picture that warms my heart. I can almost see the mountains and hear the water ripple."

"They're so alive," she replied, her voice filled with awe. "And yet, in their silence, I find a voice—one that speaks of eternal love. I realize how much the divine loves to reveal itself through nature, through these majestic mountains and tranquil lakes. Today, I felt His presence in the stillness of the water, in the whisper of the wind, in the way the mountains stand tall despite everything."

"Your journey sounds so inspiring," Arjun said, a hint of pride in his voice. "You've always had a gift for seeing the good in everything. I'm proud of you, sweetheart. And I know Riya and Aman are proud too—though they might not say it out loud."

"They are my greatest blessings," Sumati whispered, her voice heavy with emotions. "Even miles away, I feel their love guiding me. I send them my love in every breath I take here."

"Keep your heart open," Arjun replied softly. "And remember, no matter where you are in the world, you are always in our hearts. We're connected by such pure love—that no distance can diminish."

"I carry that love with me," she said, her voice catching slightly. "It's like a warm embrace that keeps me grounded and inspired. I promise to bring back stories, sketches and a renewed sense of purpose. And I can't wait to tell you all about the glaciers and the fiords tomorrow."

"Just hearing about your day makes me feel closer to you," Arjun said. "Thank you for sharing your journey with us. We're all part of your divine dance, just as you are part of ours."

"I love you all so much," Sumati whispered, her heart overflowing. "Thank you for supporting me, for trusting me and for loving me unconditionally. I feel so blessed to have you in my life—my greatest treasures."

"Same here, sweetheart," Arjun replied, a kind laugh in his voice. "Now, go enjoy the beauty around you. Take in the fresh air at every moment. We'll be here, waiting for your stories and your return."

"I will," she promised softly. "And I'll hold you all close in my heart, no matter how far I am. This journey is helping me see that true love is always within reach, just waiting to be recognized."

They shared a tender few moments more, exchanging words of love and reassurance, before ending the call. Sumati closed her eyes for a moment, feeling the warmth of her family's love seep into her soul. She looked out over the shimmering lake, whispering a silent prayer of gratitude—gratitude for her journey, for her loved ones and for the divine presence that guides us all.

As her time in New Zealand drew to a close, Sumati felt a mild bit of sadness mixed with gratitude. She had uncovered layers of her soul—discovering strength, love in nature and a sense of calm within.

Standing at the airport, she looked back at the mountains one last time, whispering a silent prayer of thanks.

"This journey has helped me realise the divine within me," she thought. "Now, I carry this light wherever I go, spreading hope and love."

With her heart full of optimism and her spirit renewed, she boarded the plane back to India. But her journey was far from over. She knew that the holy dance of life would continue, everywhere she went.

And as the plane lifted into the sky, she whispered softly, "The universe is my home and love is my guide."

CHAPTER 4

IN THE LANDS OF COLOR, SNOW AND TEMPLES

Sumati's journey from New Zealand to India was a return to her roots—a homecoming to the land of her ancestors. But, before returning to Mumbai, her heart desired more and she wanted to explore her own country.

Upon arriving in Jaipur, the Pink City, she was immediately enveloped by a kaleidoscope of colors, aromas and sounds.

The city's bustling markets, with stalls overflowing with fragrant spices, handcrafted textiles and shimmering jewelry, felt like a celebration of life. Yet, amid the chaos, her heart found serenity in the temples dedicated to Lord Vishnu and Krishna.

In the early morning hours, she visited the Birla Temple, where the air was thick with the scent of incense and the chants of devotees resonated like divine music. She closed her eyes, feeling the vibrations of faith and love. Her prayers mingled with theirs—her heart singing a melody of gratitude and hope.

"The Lord's presence is everywhere," she thought, tears of devotion shimmering in her eyes. "In every prayer, every smile, every breath—His supreme love flows through everything."

She sat in the temple courtyard, soaking in the freshness of that morning, with the cheerful chirping of the birds around her, a melody that welcomed the new day. She meditated on the amazing qualities of patience and surrender—trusting that her prayers were heard and the universe was unfolding in perfect harmony.

As the day passed, Sumati found herself wandering through a bustling street in the heart of Jaipur's old town. The air was thick with the aroma of spices—saffron, cumin, cardamom—and the sweet scent of marigolds and jasmine. The rhythmic hum of lively chatter and the clatter of bangles resonated all around her.

Soon, she was drawn to a small open square where children, their faces alight with mischief and joy, gathered to play a familiar game—hopscotch. The chalk outlines on the earth had faded over time but their laughter and innocence brought the game alive. Sumati's face lit up as she stepped into the circle, inviting a shy girl to be her partner.

"Chalo, chalo!" she exclaimed softly in Hindi, gesturing to the chalked grid. The children giggled and eagerly took her hands, guiding her through the simple sequence—one, two, three—hop, hop—landing on the numbered boxes. Their small feet jumped with glee and Sumati's heart warmed at the carefree happiness that flooded her. For a moment, she was transported back to her childhood—free of worries, immersed in the pure joys of play.

After a fun game, she sat on a low wooden bench, watching the children chase each other and exchange stories. Their wide, curious eyes reflected a world of wonder and she felt a deep sense of connection—this is the universal language of innocence and love.

Next, her footsteps led her to a bustling market stall adorned with radiant, colorful bangles. The artisan, a young man with a gentle smile, carefully arranged rows of glass, lac and metal bangles—each shimmering with intricate designs and hues ranging from fiery reds and royal blues to delicate pinks and emerald greens. Sumati's eyes sparkled as she picked up a few, listening to the chime they made when gently tapped together.

"Madam, these bangles are special," the merchant said softly. "They carry the energy of Rajasthan—bold, beautiful and full of life."

She chose a set of bright orange and fuchsia bangles for herself and a collection of smaller, delicate ones for her daughter Riya. She also selected a traditional lehenga—a long, flowing skirt embroidered with mirror work and intricate thread patterns—and a matching choli. The fabrics felt soft and luxurious, echoing the rich heritage of the land.

As she draped herself in the traditional attire, she felt a sense of belonging—a deep bond with the culture that had nurtured her and her ancestors for generations.

Eager to indulge her palate, Sumati then visited a nearby street food stall, where a woman in a colorful saree prepared local delicacies. The aroma of freshly baked bajra roti (millet bread), spicy dal, and tangy pickles wafted through the air. She ordered a plate of dal bati churma—crisp baked balls of dough served with a sweetened, crushed wheat mixture.

She savored each bite, relishing the fiery, fragrant flavors that danced on her tongue. The food was rich, hearty and full of tradition—each ingredient telling a story of Rajasthan's history, its deserts and its vibrant festivals.

As she ate, she exchanged warm smiles with the local vendors and children who gathered around, eager to share their stories and learn about her journey. Her heart swelled with gratitude for this authentic slice of Jaipur life—simple, rooted in love, culture and community.

That evening, as the sun dipped below the horizon and the city shimmered under a canopy of stars, Sumati felt a great sense of gratitude in playing with children, wearing traditional clothes and tasting the soul of Jaipur's cuisines.

Feeling refreshed, she knew these moments would stay etched in her heart forever, fueling her journey inward with the same zest and innocence she found in that lively, colorful city.

The next morning Sumati stepped out of her quaint guesthouse, her heart brimming with anticipation. The city was alive—vivid colors splashed everywhere and the lively hum of conversations, laughter and music beckoned her to dive into the heart of Jaipur's culture once again.

Her first destination today was the famous Hawa Mahal, the "Palace of Winds," its honeycomb façade shimmering in unique shades of pink as the sunlight danced upon its intricate latticework. Sumati marveled at the honeycomb windows, designed to allow royal women to observe street festivals while remaining unseen. She pressed her hand gently against the cool stone, feeling the history and the secrets it held.

As she wandered around the palace's sprawling courtyards, she was caught up in a spontaneous fair of sounds. Street vendors called out their wares—jewellery, brass items and sweets.

She stopped at a small shop adorned with handwoven textiles, where a cheerful shopkeeper named Mohan caught her attention. His face was radiating warmth and his hands moved skilfully as he arranged bright fabrics and embroidery.

"Madam, welcome!" he greeted kindly. "Are you looking for something special today?"

"Yes," Sumati replied with a smile. "I want to experience the true colors of Jaipur—its fabrics, its crafts, its essence. Tell me about your work."

Mohan's eyes sparkled as he beckoned her inside. "Come, I will show you something very special—our traditional Bandhani work, a craft passed down through generations. It's a dyeing technique unique to Rajasthan, creating intricate patterns with tiny, tied knots of fabric."

Sumati's curiosity deepened. "I've heard of Bandhani, but I've never seen it in action. Please, tell me more."

Mohan nodded eagerly. "Bandhani is more than a craft—it's a story woven into every thread. We tie small sections of fabric tightly with thread, then dye the cloth in vibrant colors. When the knots are removed, beautiful patterns—dots, waves, geometric shapes—appear. Each design has its own meaning and significance—wishes for prosperity, love, or good health."

He reached into a drawer and pulled out a beautifully dyed piece of fabric—deep maroon with tiny white dots, forming a mesmerizing pattern. "This one is called 'Shikari,' symbolizing the hunter's courage. And this green one with yellow dots is for celebrations, for joy and abundance on the festival of 'Teej'.

Sumati's eyes widened with admiration. "It's like capturing the soul of Rajasthan in fabric. Such delicate work—how long does it take to make these?"

"Ah, it depends on the complexity," Mohan said with a grin. "A simple piece can take a day or two but more intricate designs may take weeks. Every dot, every pattern is a labor of love and patience."

She was captivated. "I'd love to see the process—can I try tying a few knots myself?"

Mohan chuckled. "Of course! Come, I'll teach you. It's simple but requires patience and steady hands."

He led her to the back of the shop, where colorful fabrics and threads were neatly arranged. He handed her a small square of cloth and a spool of thread. Carefully, he showed her how to pinch tiny sections of fabric, twist and tie them securely with fine threads.

As she attempted to imitate his movements, her fingers fumbled at first—her knots were uneven and some threads slipped—but her smile didn't fade. Mohan laughed kindly. "That's the spirit! Every knot is a step closer to creating wonder."

For a while, they worked together, her hands moving in rhythm with the gentle hum of the city outside. Sumati's eyes lit up with joy—this was more than an artisan's craft; it was a skill of tradition, patience and love.

After her little lesson, she selected a few pieces—richly dyed fabrics with bold patterns—and bought them as souvenirs. Mohan wrapped them carefully, tying a small red thread around each one, blessing them with good wishes.

"Madam," he said with a wide smile, "these fabrics carry the spirit of Jaipur—full of life, color, and hope. Wear them with pride or gift them to loved ones and may they bring happiness."

"Thank you, Mohan," Sumati said warmly. "Your craft is truly magical. I will cherish these and tell everyone I meet about your beautiful work."

As she stepped out of the shop, her arms full of colorful fabrics, her heart was light with joy. The city's colors had seeped into her soul—vivid, lively, full of stories waiting to be told.

Her next stop was a visit to the famous Jal Mahal, the Water Palace, set amidst the Mansagar Lake. She marveled at its ethereal beauty—its pink façade shimmering under the afternoon sun as water lilies floated nearby. She wandered along the lakeshore, watching fishermen casting their nets and children splashing in the shallow waters.

Suddenly, the air filled with the sound of traditional Rajasthani folk music—lutes, flutes and drums—emanating from a nearby courtyard. Drawn by the melody, Sumati found herself in the midst of a lively celebration: a local festival of colors and dance.

Women in ghagras twirled in unison, their skirts swirling in reds, blues and yellows, while men played drums and sang hearty folk songs. Children ran around with painted faces, chasing each other with colored powders. The scene was pure joy—an explosion of life, laughter and love.

Sumati couldn't resist joining the festivities. She picked up a handful of bright colored powders, laughing as she smeared them on her cheeks and arms. She spun with the children, her ghagra swirling in the air, feeling more alive than ever.

In the middle of the celebration, a group of musicians invited her to dance. She accepted eagerly, her feet moving spontaneously to the infectious rhythm. Her heart soared—this was the true essence of Jaipur, a city that celebrated life in every hue and every beat.

As the sun began to set, casting a warm glow over the city, Sumati felt a deep sense of gratitude. She realized that Jaipur's true magic was in its ability to make everyone feel part of its vibrant tapestry—a place where tradition and joy thrived side by side.

Later that evening, she found herself sitting on the rooftop terrace of her guesthouse, sipping chai and watching the city lights flicker on like stars fallen from the sky. Her heart was full—filled with the sights, sounds and stories of Jaipur's soul.

Her mind replayed the day's adventures—the laughter with children, the intricate art of Bandhani, the joy of dancing in the festival and the kindness of Mohan, the craftsman who shared his craft with such pride. She felt a deep connection to the city, its colors, its traditions, its heartbeat.

Her spirit was alive with inspiration. She knew these memories—the fun filled moments and interactions—would stay with her forever, fueling her inner journey of love and discovery.

She closed her eyes for a moment, breathing in the warm night air and whispered softly:

"Thank you, Jaipur, for showing me that life's true colors are found in joy, patience and love."

With her heart open and her soul enriched, Sumati eagerly looked forward to the next chapter of her journey—knowing that every moment, every experience, was a thread woven into the divinity of her life.

From Jaipur, Sumati travelled north to Kashmir (Srinagar)—the land of eternal snow and splendid scenery. The moment she stepped into Srinagar, the serenity of the Dal Lake and the snow-capped Himalayas took her breath away.

She visited the Shankaracharya Temple, perched high on a hill overlooking the lake. The temple's ancient stones echoed with the chants of pilgrims seeking the Lord's blessings. As she bowed her head before the deity, she felt an overwhelming sense of his sublime presence—like a warm embrace from the Lord Himself.

Walking along the floating markets and gardens, she marvelled at the intricate craftsmanship of Kashmiri shawls and carpets. She browsed through an array of shops selling handcrafted paper mache items. But what touched her most was the unwavering faith of the local people—who still continued living in Kashmir, bound by the belief that someday their state would shine in communal unity.

One evening, she sat by the lake at dusk, watching the reflection of the mountains shimmer on the water. She closed her eyes, whispering a prayer for joy and love to all beings.

"In this sacred land," she thought, "Divinity is woven into every stone, every prayer, every smile. The Lord's grace is evident in every corner of this earth and no wonder it was once referred to as Paradise on Earth".

During her stay in Kashmir, Sumati was invited to participate in a local festival honoring the divine. As she entered the temple, she witnessed a miraculous event—an elderly devotee, who had been blind for years, suddenly opened his eyes during the prayer. The crowds watched in hushed awe. A collective gasp swept through the assembly. Finally, the entire community erupted in joy, believing it to be a divine blessing. The villagers, witnessing this, fell to their knees in prayer. The old man's eyes, once clouded, now shimmered with a brilliant, unmistakable light. Tears streamed down his face as he looked around in wonder—at the glowing faces of loved ones, the vibrant colors of the temple and the distant mountains bathed in the dying sunlight.

He turned his gaze upward, as if seeing the sky for the first time, and whispered softly, "I can see… I see… the light." His voice was filled with emotion and disbelief. His eyes, filled with tears of joy, reflected a universe of divine grace.

Sumati's heart too was brimming with joy. She saw in that moment the power of unwavering belief and divine grace. Her own belief grew stronger, anchored by the miracle she had witnessed.

"The Lord's miracles are all around us," she thought, her eyes shining. "We only need to open our hearts and believe."

That night, she meditated under the starlit sky, feeling God's presence in every breath, every star and every whisper of the wind.

In Kashmir’s tranquil surroundings, Sumati’s optimism blossomed anew. She realized that her belief was a luminous thread connecting her to the Lord—giving her strength, courage and joy.

"Where I go, she thought, the Lord’s light guides through, an eternal light guiding me home".

Next morning the sun cast a gentle lemon hue over Srinagar as Sumati prepared for her temporary departure. The city with its shimmering Dal Lake and bustling markets, had been her home for days, but now her heart yearned for the serenity of the hills and the quiet beauty of Pehelgam. She packed her small bag carefully, ensuring she had her favorite shawl, her notebook and a few personal mementos. Her mind replayed the conversations she’d had with locals, the scent of saffron and jasmine in the air and the gentle lapping of the lake against the shikaras.

As she stepped into the cool morning air, a sense of calm washed over her. The drive from Srinagar to Pehelgam was a scenic journey; lush green fields stretched endlessly, dotted with vibrant flowers and distant snow-capped peaks. The hills around Pehelgam, with their undulating contours and dense coniferous forests, seemed to beckon her into a world untouched by time.

Arriving at Pehelgam, Sumati felt a rush of adrenaline. The mountain air was crisp and invigorating, filling her lungs with freshness. She checked into a charming guesthouse nestled amongst towering pine trees, their branches whispering in the breeze. Her first step outside was to the edge of the lake, a mirror of tranquillity framed by the hills.

The lake's surface shimmered under the sun, inviting her to indulge in a simple pleasure she cherished since childhood—playing with pebbles. She sat on a smooth stone by the water's edge, her fingers tracing the cool, rounded stones. Memories flooded her mind—how she used to gather pebbles as a child, skipping stones across the water, watching the ripples expand outward. She chuckled softly, realizing how little had changed. The joy of those simple acts still held a magic that no worldly trouble could diminish.

Sumati spent hours by the lake, her eyes tracing the silhouettes of the hills and the distant mountains. The landscape was enchanting—verdant meadows dotted with wildflowers, and the sound of distant waterfalls adding a soothing melody to the scenery. She felt a deep connection to this place, as if the hills were whispering stories she longed to hear.

During her exploration, she encountered a local family—an elderly couple and their young daughter. Their warm smiles and genuine hospitality immediately drew her in. They welcomed her like an old friend, offering her traditional Kashmiri tea—kahwa—rich with saffron, almonds and cinnamon. The aroma was enticing, evoking memories of her childhood and the warmth of her own family.

As they sat together on a wooden veranda overlooking the lake, the family insisted she stay for a meal. Their humble home was filled with the pungent smell of spices and freshly cooked dishes. She tasted the traditional Kashmiri wazwan—a sumptuous spread of rice, vegetables and tender meat, seasoned with herbs and spices that danced on her palate. The family's daughter, a bright-eyed girl named Amina, eagerly explained the significance of each dish, her voice bubbly with pride.

While sharing the meal, Sumati learned about their lives, their hopes, and their love for the land. They talked about the hills, the changing seasons and the importance of preserving their traditions. The family's warmth and generosity touched her deeply, reminding her of the simple joys that make life meaningful—the kindness of strangers, the glory of nature and the comfort of shared stories.

Before she left, the family presented her with a small, handcrafted bat made of 'Sheesham' wood for her son Aman. Sumati knew Aman would love it.. She promised to keep it safe for him, imagining his delight at receiving such a thoughtful gift. As a token of remembrance, she bought a beautifully embroidered shawl from their village, which she knew would remind her of this warm encounter whenever she wore it.

The family then took her on a sightseeing tour through the surrounding hills. They showed her the scenic meadows where herds of sheep grazed merrily, the ancient temples carved into the rocky outcrops and the vibrant markets bustling with local artisans. They took her to a viewpoint overlooking the valley, where the landscape unfolded like a living painting—rolling hills, lush forests, and the distant snow-capped peaks touching the sky.

Throughout the day, Sumati felt her heart fill with gratitude. The kindness of this family, their stories and the breathtaking scenery had woven themselves into her memories. She realized that travel was more than just seeing new places—it was about connecting with people, understanding their lives and finding echoes of her own dreams and memories.

As the sun began to set, casting a warm caramel glow over the mountains, she bid farewell to her new friends. With a content heart, she returned to her guesthouse, her mind filled with the serenity of Pehelgam and the warmth of human connection.

The next morning, after a leisurely breakfast, Sumati took one last walk along the lake. She paused to touch the pebbles once more, watching the ripples spread across the water—reminding her that life, like those pebbles, was about making gentle impacts, creating fun in small acts. She took a deep breath, inhaling the crisp, pine-scented air and felt a profound sense of calm.

As she prepared to leave Pehelgam and return to Srinagar, she carried with her not just souvenirs and gifts, but a renewed spirit. The hills, the lake and her new friends had gifted her a reminder of life's simple pleasures—the kindness of strangers, the beauty of nature and the importance of holding onto one's childhood joy.

The journey back was equally scenic, with the mountains gradually giving way to the bustling cityscape of Srinagar. Yet, inside her, a quiet glow persisted. She knew that Pehelgam had left an indelible mark on her soul and that the memories of the hills, the lake, and the warm Kashmiri family would always be cherished by her.

After her rejuvenating days in Kashmir, immersed in the tranquil beauty of the mountains and the sacred whispers of the lakes, Sumati felt a gentle pull towards the next chapter of her spiritual quest. With renewed devotion and gratitude, she boarded a flight southward, leaving the snow-capped peaks behind. Her destination was Varanasi—the eternal city of the Ganges—where the river's holy flow would deepen her connection to the divine and guide her further on her journey inward.

The early morning mist hovered over Varanasi like a gentle shroud, cloaking the city in an aura of mysticism. Sumati stepped out of her humble guesthouse, feeling the cool, sacred air seep into her bones. She was drawn to the ghats—the steps leading down to the river—where the city's heartbeat pulsed strongest.

Varanasi was in her soul. The aroma of incense, the chants echoing from distant temples, the scent of marigolds and sandalwood—all woven into the fabric of her being. The city's holiness was palpable, a living, breathing testament to centuries of devotion.

Sumati's heart was brimming with reverence as she approached the Kashi Vishwanath Temple, one of the most sacred shrines dedicated to Lord Shiva. She bowed deeply on the cool marble floor, lighting a ghee lamp and offering her prayers with pure devotion.

"Om Namah Shivaya," she whispered, feeling the sacred mantra resonate within her. She closed her eyes, surrendering her worries, her restless longing into the divine. Her prayers rose like fragrant smoke, merging with the prayers of countless devotees.

Next, she visited the nearby temple of Goddess Parvati, feeling her presence envelop her in true love. She poured out her heart, seeking strength, clarity and devotion. Her love for the Almighty deepened as she felt the gentle touch of Parvati's compassion, the fierce strength of Shiva's serenity.

Walking through the bustling streets, Sumati encountered ascetics—sadhus adorned in saffron robes, their hair matted and dreadlocked, faces etched with wisdom and tranquillity. Some sat in deep meditation, others offering blessings to passing pilgrims with serene smiles.

She approached a wise sadhu, whose eyes sparkled with immense knowledge. They exchanged stories—his tales of renunciation, of finding divine bliss in austerity and her stories of her journey across India and beyond.

The sadhu's charm lay in his unshakable calm, a reminder of the eternal truth beyond worldly illusions. She felt humbled and inspired, realizing that true devotion was an unwavering surrender to the divine.

He looked no more than thirty, but his face told stories of countless lifetimes of devotion. His skin was a warm, earthy brown, marked with lines that seemed carved by the wind and the sun. His eyes were deep-set, dark, and luminous—a gaze that appeared to hold the knowledge of ages, yet shone with a gentle, childlike innocence.

His hair was long, unkempt and matted, falling in tangled black strands that framed his face and shoulders. A thin, saffron-colored cloth wrapped around his waist, the fabric faded from years of sun and rain. Over his shoulders, he draped a simple, worn shawl—frayed at the edges but carefully kept, as if it carried the memories of his spiritual journey. Around his neck hung a rudraksha mala, beads worn smooth by countless prayers.

He sat motionless, eyes closed for a moment, then opened them slowly to reveal a calm, unwavering gaze. His face was serene, almost ethereal, as if he was tuned to a different plane of existence—the divine presence he sought to blend with.

Sumati hesitated for a moment, then approached softly. "Namaste," she said quietly, bowing her head.

He looked up at her, a faint smile touching his lips. "Namaste," he replied, his voice gentle, yet imbued with a deep strength.

"Who are you?" she asked, her voice tinged with curiosity and reverence. "And what brings you here, sitting so carefree by the river?"

He paused, then answered simply, "I am a sadhu. A seeker on the path to merging with the divine. I have chosen these ghats as my sacred place, for the Ganges is the mother of all purifications. Here, I find the space to prepare for my final journey."

Her eyes lingered on him, sensing an extraordinary depth. "You seem so young," she remarked softly. "What has led you to this path at such a young age?"

He looked at her with gentle eyes, a trace of a smile lingering. "Life has taught me many lessons—pleasure and pain, hope and despair. The river has shown me that everything is transient. To truly find peace, one must surrender and become one with the divine, like the flowing water that merges with the ocean. I have been seeking that union, and now I feel my time has come to become one with the Lord, to dissolve into the infinite."

There was a stillness about him that transcended age or appearance. It was as if he had already touched eternity and now only waited for the final moment to fully dissolve into it.

"What is your purpose here?" she asked softly.

"To prepare my soul," he replied. "I meditate continuously, surrendering my ego, my desires, my fears. I chant the Lord's name—Hari, Ram, Shiva—whatever feels most divine. I am here to blend into the Supreme consciousness, to become a part of the eternal truth."

She looked at him, awe-struck by his calm acceptance. ?" " Why do you think of death?" she asked.

He shook his head gently. "Death is just a doorway, a passage to another state of being. When one has realized the divine within, death loses its sting. It is not an end but a merging, a return to the source from which we came."

His words resonated deeply within her, stirring a sense of humility and reverence. "And what do you leave behind?" she whispered.

He smiled softly. "Love. Compassion. The remembrance that every soul is divine and every moment is sacred. My only wish is that others may also realize their true nature before it is time to depart."

As the morning sun climbed higher, warming the cool breeze, the sadhu closed his eyes again, resuming his meditative posture. His breathing continued to be rhythmic.

Sumati sat quietly beside him, feeling the profound calm that radiated from his being. She realized that in this moment, she was witnessing a soul preparing for its sacred journey—an inspiring reminder of the impermanence of life and the eternal nature of the divine.

When she finally stood to leave, she gently spoke "May your journey be blessed," she whispered, her voice almost choking.

He opened his eyes once more, looking at her with love and kindness. “May you find your own divine path,” he replied softly. “Remember, the Lord dwells within us all—just listen and you will hear the eternal song.”

As Sumati turned to leave the ghats, she carried the serenity of that moment in her heart, knowing she had witnessed a sacred transition— a reminder that life’s ultimate purpose was to realize the divine within.

As the day went on, Sumati boarded a small, weathered boat, its wooden planks creaking softly beneath her. The boatman, an elderly man with a gentle smile, guided her across the sacred Ganges.

The river was alive—pilgrims bathing in its holy waters, priests performing rituals on the ghats, children playing with the rippling waves. The Ganges Mother was majestic, her waters shimmering with the morning light, reflecting countless temples and the floating diyas (oil lamps).

Sumati closed her eyes as the boat floated gently. She felt the divine presence of the Ganges—Mother Ganga herself—her warm, nourishing embrace washing away all doubts and fears. She whispered a prayer for her family, for herself, for her journey and for the world.

As the boat reached the opposite bank, Sumati stepped onto the sacred ground once more, her heart filled with a profound sense of devotion. She had come seeking answers, but found more—an awakening of her inner divine spirit.

Sitting quietly on the riverbank, she watched the sky, resembling a silken canvas in gold and cool blues. Her mind was tranquil and clear. The Ganges had cleansed her heart and she knew she was forever connected to this loving mother's eternal flow.

In that moment, she felt a deep satisfaction—an understanding that her journey was not just about discovering the world but about reconnecting with her inner divine, the divine within all.

As evening fell, Sumati prepared to leave Varanasi, her spirit renewed and her devotion deepened. She knew her next destination was Mumbai, where her loved ones awaited her. Her heart now carried the sacred memories of Varanasi—its holiness, the ascetics' charm, the Ganges' blessing.

She was ready to return, carrying the immeasurable love she had gathered, eager to share her newfound calm with her family and her city.

CHAPTER 5

THE JOY OF HOMECOMING

After days of wandering through distant lands—immersing herself in the sacred mountains of Kashmir, the tranquil lakes of New Zealand, the vibrant streets of Jaipur, the sacredness of the wonderful Varanasi and the spiritual depths of her own soul—Sumati finally steps back into Mumbai. The familiar noise of the city welcomes her like an old friend, yet she feels fundamentally transformed. Her eyes sparkle with new learnings, her heart resonates with divine love and her spirit carries the stories of her odyssey.

As her train pulls into Chhatrapati Shivaji Station, she pauses for a moment on the platform, absorbing the sights, sounds and scents of home. The bustling crowd, the honking autos, the aroma of street food—these are the threads woven into her tapestry of belonging. She feels a deep, peaceful gratitude—her journey has led her to rediscover her roots, not as a place of origin only, but as a wellspring of love, strength and inspiration.

As the evening Sun dipped behind the horizon, casting a golden hue over the bustling courtyard, Sumati's heart fluttered in quiet anticipation.

Stepping into her cozy home, Sumati is greeted by her eagerly waiting husband Arjun—also an artist, whose big, round eyes are expressing a hearty welcome—and her children, Riya and Aman, whose innocent laughter fills the air with pure joy. Their warm hugs envelop her like a comforting embrace, dissolving the fatigue of her travels. Her children's curious eyes drink in her stories, her smile, her aura of serenity and vitality.

Arjun, holding her hand, whispers softly, "Welcome back, my love. You've journeyed across the world, I see the happy glint in your beautiful eyes, shining brighter than ever." Their love, rooted in understanding and mutual respect, now feels even deeper—strengthened by her many voyages and her renewed sense of purpose.

Their reunion was gentle yet profound. No grand declarations, just the soft brush of hands, a knowing smile, and the warmth of two souls who had journeyed far yet remained forever intertwined. Arjun's touch was tender, a whisper of love that had endured the test of time, now renewed with a deeper, more realistic connection.

Sumati felt her heart swell— upon seeing her pet 'Sasha,' her love, her confidant—standing before her, a fluffy, Golden retriever. Their love was a quiet symphony, built on years of companionship and fun filled moments. Sumati's eyes glisten with tears of gratitude. She had traveled across mountains and sacred rivers, seeking the only truth and was now over the moon coming back home, being reunited with her beloved—her partner, her children, her 'Sasha'—whose presence filled her with a renewed sense of purpose and joy.

The next afternoon, her dear friend Anjali arrives at her doorstep, her eyes bright with excitement. Accompanying her is her husband, Rohan and both are eager to hear about her adventures. Anjali, with a warm smile, presents Sumati with a vibrant bouquet of continental, pink lilies – a token of celebration and good wishes.

As they settle into Sumati's cozy living room, the atmosphere is light and joyful. Rohan shares stories of their own travels and they all laugh over shared memories and dreams. Sumati speaks softly about her encounters—her lessons from the Kashmiri family, the learned ascetic and the importance of surrender and compassion. Her words appear to be resonating with everyone present.

The day becomes a delightful exchange of stories, hopes and reflections. It is more than just a celebration; it is a reaffirmation of friendship and camaraderie.

In the evenings post Sumati's return, the family gathers around her—listening with rapt attention as Sumati shares tales of her adventures, the sacred encounters, the lessons learned from nature's ethereal dance. Her stories are infused with wonder and gratitude, inspiring her children to see the divine in every moment.

In that moment, under the star-studded sky, surrounded by the warmth of family and the blessings of the universe, Sumati realizes that love's greatest beauty lay not only in grand gestures but in the simple, sacred joys of being truly seen and cherished by the ones who genuinely love her. Her journey had led her across the world but her greatest discovery was the profound love she shares with Arjun—a love that, like the eternal river of Ganges, flowed deep and unending, nourishing their hearts and binding them forever.

As they embrace, the world around them shimmered with hope and promise, a testament to the enduring power of love, devotion and the sacred joy of coming home.

Back in Arjun's art studio, canvases burst with vibrant colors—mountains shimmering with spiritual light, lakes reflecting the vast universe, temples alive with devotion. He begins to paint the reflections of Sumati's journey, his brush capturing not just landscapes but even the great emotions of awe, humility and love she experienced. His paintings become a visual symphony of Sumati's inner ponderings and learnings.

Simultaneously, Sumati's writing blossoms. Sumati begins composing her memoir—a poetic biography titled "Return to the Heart". It narrates her journey from the restless city girl to an explorer artist and inspired writer. She describes her encounters with tribes, her meditations amidst pristine nature, the miracles she witnessed and the divine love she discovered within herself.

The book resonates deeply with readers. Its lyrical prose, authentic experiences and vivid imagery quickly make it a bestseller. Critics praise her for her heartfelt storytelling, her ability to weave the wonders of nature into everyday life and her inspiring message of hope and sublime connection. Readers from across India and beyond write to her, sharing how her journey has touched their hearts and rekindled their belief. She is humbled.

At her book launch, surrounded by friends, family and fans, Sumati feels a wave of gratitude. Her voice crackles with emotion as she thanks everyone who supported her—her family for their unwavering love, her readers for their trust and the Lord for guiding her.

She reflects: "This success is not mine alone. It's a reflection of the divine dance within us. I am merely a vessel, sharing the universal love I've found on my journey."

Her family's pride and love shine brightly. Arjun presents her with a new canvas— a letter addressed to her which he had written while she was away. It speaks of his profound love for her and elaborates the days he spent in her remembrance.

Sumati's homecoming is not just a return to physical space but a celebration of her inner journey. Her story becomes a beacon for others—showing that the true journey is inward and that supreme love is always accessible.

Her life now embodies the harmony of physical, spiritual and cosmic love—an ongoing odyssey rooted in gratitude, faith and self-discovery. She continues to paint and write and is ever grateful for the divine dance that brought her home—to herself, to her family and to the universe.

One Sunday evening, as her family gathers in the living room, Sumati opens her latest journal. She writes simply:

“Life is a divine dance—each step, each breath, each heartbeat a rhythm of love. My journey has shown me that home is not just a place but a state of being—connected to the Lord within and all around. I am finally home, in the eternal embrace of love, I am non-existent and only God is".

With her heart overflowing, she looks out of the window at the amber and blue Mumbai skyline, the stars glittering above—reminding her that her odyssey is never truly over. Every living moment is a new beginning, a new step into the wonders of life.

In this joyful homecoming, Sumati finds her true happiness—not just in worldly success or recognition but in the deep sense of love, acceptance and harmony that now fills her life. Her story inspires us all to listen to the whisper of the universe within and to embrace the divine that connects us all.

JIST OF SUMATI'S ITINERARY

Step 1.
02 Oct 2024
Mumbai – New Zealand
Flight –
Australian airways (name changed)
Mumbai – Queenstown, NZ
23 hrs 25 min (with 2 lay overs)

Stop 1.
Mumbai – Singapore
6 hrs 10 min

Stop 2.
Singapore – Sydney
7 hrs 40 min

Final
Sydney – Queenstown, Nz.
2 hr 55 min

Step 2.
12 Oct, 2024
Nz to India (Jaipur).

Flight –
Jet set airways (name changed)
25 hrs 55 min (with 2 layovers)

Stop 1.
Queenstown – Melbourne
3 hrs 25 min

Stop 2.
Melbourne – New Delhi
12 hrs 45 min

13th – 14th Oct Oct, 2024
New Delhi – Jaipur
Air local (name changed)
1 hr

Step 3.
Jaipur to Kashmir –
18th oct
Flight
Air Express(name changed) – 3 hr 33 min

Stop 1.
Jaipur – New Delhi
1 hr
New Delhi – Srinagar
1 hr 40 min

Step 4.
Kashmir to Varanasi
22nd Oct, 2024
Flight
Imicon (name changed) – 4 hrs 33 min with 1 stop

Stop 1.
Srinagar to New Delhi
1 hr 45 min

New Delhi – Varanasi
1 hr 35 min

Step 5.
Varanasi to Mumbai
Train
29th October 2024
JST EXPRESS (11049) (name changed)

A SUMMARY OF SUMATI'S JOURNAL

Experiences and Lessons

1. Inner calm is the true treasure

Experience:

During her meditation by the tranquil lakes in New Zealand, Sumati realized that true serenity comes from within. Sitting silently amidst the mountains, she felt a deep connection to the divine rhythm of nature, understanding that peace is a state of inner harmony rather than external circumstances.

Lesson:

Cultivating inner calm. External chaos and worldly pursuits are fleeting but the calm rooted in the divine essence of the self offers lasting fulfillment. Regular meditation and mindfulness help us reconnect with that core of tranquility, making us resilient to life's ups and downs.

2. Nature as a Divine Mirror

Experience:

Sumati's treks through Fiordland, the mountains of Kashmir and her moments beside lakes revealed that nature embodies divine energy. The whispering winds, cascading waterfalls and luminous lakes reflected the qualitie of love and harmony.

Lesson:

Nature is a sacred teacher and a mirror of our inner universe. Living holistically involves respecting and nurturing our environment, recognizing that we are an integral part of this divine ecosystem. By observing and learning from nature's many wonders, we discover our alignment with the divine.

3. Trust in Divine Timing and Guidance

Experience:

Throughout her travels—from the mountains of Kashmir to the sacred city of Varanasi—Sumati faced uncertainties and moments of doubt. Yet, each time she surrendered her fears and trusted the divine flow, she experienced miraculous moments—like the healing of the blind devotee or the serenity of her mountain meditations.

Lesson:

Living with belief means trusting that the universe unfolds in divine timing. When we surrender control and listen inwardly, guidance and miracles become visible. Believing in divine guidance creates space for grace to enter our lives.

4. Love is the Foundation of a Holistic Life

Experience:

Sumati's interactions with her family, her encounters with the Maori elders, and the acts of kindness in Jaipur and Kashmir revealed that love connects everything. Her children's innocence, her husband's gentle support and her compassion for others demonstrated that love is a universal force.

Lesson:

Unconditional love—toward oneself, others and nature. Love nurtures our emotional, spiritual and physical well being. When we live with love as our guiding principle, we foster harmony and healing in all aspects of life.

5. Embrace and Celebrate Cultural and Spiritual Diversity

Experience:

Her journey through different lands exposed her to diverse cultures—Maori, Kashmiri, Rajasthani and others—each with unique spiritual practices and traditions. She learned from their deep-rooted faith and respect for nature.

Lesson:

Openness and respect for different spiritual paths. Embracing diversity enriches our understanding of the divine and broadens our perspective. Every culture offers unique lessons on love, patience, surrender and harmony, which collectively deepen our spiritual journey.

6. Healing Comes Through Faith and Divine Grace

Experience:

The miraculous event in Kashmir where the old man's eyesight was restored was a pivotal moment for Sumati. Witnessing divine grace in action reaffirmed her belief that faith can catalyze healing—both physical and emotional.

Lesson:

Holistic living includes trusting in divine grace for healing and growth. When we strengthen our faith and surrender to divine will, we open ourselves to miracles—healing wounds, overcoming fears and awakening inner strength.

7. Living in the Present Moment

Experience:

Sumati's deep connection with the lakes, mountains and temples in New Zealand and Kashmir taught her the importance of being fully present. Her awareness of the divine energy flowing in each moment made her realize that life's beauty unfolds in the now.

Lesson:

Life is rooted in mindfulness—being present with what is, without attachment to the past or anxiety about the future.

This awareness allows us to experience life's divine wonders and love fully, cultivating gratitude and serenity.

8. Self-Discovery Is a Sacred Journey

Experience:

Her travels to distant lands and her moments of solitude revealed layers of her inner self. Journaling her thoughts and meditating in nature led her to uncover her innate spiritual strength and creative talents.

Lesson:

Embracing self-awareness and self-acceptance. Every experience, joyful or challenging, is an opportunity for inner growth. Self-discovery deepens our understanding of divine purpose, guiding us to live authentically.

9. Acts of Kindness and Service Nourish the Soul

Experience:

Volunteering in the community garden in New Zealand and sharing smiles with children in Jaipur reminded her that service is a divine act. These simple acts foster love, compassion and a sense of unity.

Lesson:

Holistic living involves serving others with kindness, recognizing that every act of love plants seeds of more love in the world. Service enhances our sense of interconnectedness and enriches our soul's journey.

10. Patience and Resilience Are Divine Virtues

Experience:

Climbing the mountains of Remarkables and trekking through dense forests taught her patience and resilience. Each challenge she faced became a spiritual lesson—like the mountains that stood tall despite storms.

Lesson:

Cultivating patience and resilience, trusting that difficulties are opportunities to strengthen our inner character. These qualities are divine virtues that help us navigate life's inevitable storms with grace.

11. Surrender and Trust Lead to Divine Miracles

Experience:

The moment in Kashmir when the blind man's eyesight was restored exemplified surrender—trusting the divine absolutely can lead to the miraculous. Her own act of surrender in meditation opened her to great insights.

Lesson:

Life is about surrendering the ego's need to control and trusting divine wisdom. This surrender creates space for divine miracles to manifest and life to flow effortlessly.

12. Living with Gratitude Opens the Heart

Experience:

Every moment—whether watching a sunset in New Zealand, tasting Rajasthani food or witnessing a miracle—filled her with thankfulness.

Lesson:

A grateful heart is receptive to divine blessings. Practicing gratitude shifts focus from lack to abundance, fostering joy, love and holistic well-being.

13. Balance Is Essential—Body, Mind and Spirit

Experience:

Sumati balanced her physical activities—trekking, volunteering, exploring—with spiritual practices—meditation, prayer, reflection. This harmony nurtured her overall well-being.

Lesson:

Attending to our health, mental clarity and spiritual growth. When these aspects are aligned, life becomes a seamless dance of love.

14. Love Is the Divine's Most Powerful Expression

Experience:

Her interactions with her children, her husband and the Maori elders showed her that love is the divine's purest form. Her deep bond with her family and her acts of kindness reflected this truth.

Lesson:

Living with love as the foundation transforms ordinary moments into sacred experiences. Love heals, unites and elevates us.

15. Acceptance and Surrender Bring Peace

Experience:

In Kashmir, when she saw the miracle of the old man's restored sight, she understood that surrendering to divine will brings healing beyond understanding.

Lesson:

Acceptance of life's divine plan reduces suffering and opens the heart to divine grace. Surrendering attachments and outcomes allows us to flow with the divine plan without doubts.

16. Faith Converts Challenges into Opportunities

Experience:

Facing uncertainties in her journey, Sumati learned to see obstacles as divine lessons. Her faith turned setbacks into opportunities for spiritual growth.

Lesson:

Cultivating unwavering faith that every experience, good or bad, is part of the divine plan. This perspective transforms challenges into catalysts for inner evolution.

17. Every Moment Is Sacred—Find the Divine in Daily Life

Experience:

From the simple joy of playing with children in Jaipur to the sacred rituals in Varanasi, she realized that God's presence permeates every moment.

Lesson:

Recognizing the sacredness of everyday life—every breath, every smile, every act of kindness is a divine offering. Living consciously transforms mundane moments into sacred experiences.

18. Humility and Gratitude Deepen Our Connection to God in our hearts

Experience:

Her encounters with wise sadhus and Maori elders taught her humility—the recognition that wisdom is infinite and accessible to everybody. We just need to open our hearts and minds.

Lesson:

Living with humility opens us to divine guidance. When we acknowledge our limitations and thank the divine for every blessing, we sense our connection deepening.

19. Creative Expression as a Path to Spiritual Fulfillment

Experience:

Sumati's art and writing became outlets for her spiritual insights. Her paintings and memoir reflected her inner journey and connected her with others.

Lesson:

Expressing our nature creatively—through art, music, writing or any heartfelt activity.

20. Love and Belief Are the Eternal Anchors

Experience:

Her journey demonstrated that love and faith are unshakeable pillars—whether witnessing miracles or embracing loved ones. These qualities sustained her through every step.

Lesson:

Living with unwavering love and belief anchors us in divine truth, providing strength, hope and resilience amid life's ebb and flow.

21. Warm and genuine hospitality

Experience:

The serene embrace of Kashmir's mountains and tranquil Dal Lake, Sumati's encounter with the warm-hearted Kashmiri family-she was welcomed with genuine kindness and humility.

Lesson:

She realized that true happiness lies in authentic human connections, compassion and reverence for nature and tradition. That unconditional hospitality was truly a gift.

Conclusion

Sumati's odyssey taught her that living life holistically is a sacred art—an ongoing dance of love, gratitude and surrender. Her experiences illuminated that the divine resides within us and everywhere around us, waiting to be recognized and embraced. By cultivating inner peace, respecting nature, trusting divine guidance and living with unconditional love, we align ourselves with the universal rhythm of life.

Her journey underscores that true happiness is not found in external achievements or possessions but in nurturing our connection to God. Every challenge, every moment of joy and every act of kindness becomes a sacred step toward realizing our highest self.

In essence, Sumati learned that life is a joyful dance—when we live with faith, love, humility and gratitude, we participate in the eternal rhythm of the universe, experiencing the divine presence in every breath, every heart beat and every moment of love. This holistic approach transforms life into a sacred journey—a continuous odyssey into the depths of our own nature.

Notes